JUST ONE DAY

A play about sexual violence and the F word

by Catherine Kay

Published by Playdead Press 2013

© Catherine Kay

Catherine Kay has asserted her rights under the Copyright, Design and Patents Act, 1988, to be identified as the author of this work.

A CIP catalogue record for this book is available from the British Library.

ISBN 978-0-9572859-7-2

Caution
All rights whatsoever in this play are strictly reserved and application for performance should be sought through the author before rehearsals begin. No performance may be given unless a license has been obtained.

This book is sold subject to the condition that it shall not by way of trade or otherwise, be lent, resold, hired out, or otherwise circulated without the publisher's prior consent in any form of binding or cover other than that in which it is published and without a similar condition including this condition being imposed on the subsequent purchaser.

Playdead Press
www.playdeadpress.com

Just One Day was first performed by Happy Theatre Collective on 29th September, 2011 at the Lowry Studio Theatre. The cast was as follows:

Shona Hurst	Rebecca Blackshaw
Janet Sparks	Catherine Kay
Sheldon Lewis	Jill Angel
Girl 29	Mary Hooten
Gary Bond	Clay Whitter
Neil Grimes	Patrick Lally
The Mother	Jill Malloy
The Father	Mark Sheals
The Boy/Policeman	Simon Mayne

Director	Helen Parry
Stage Manager/ Set Design/Costume/ Make Up	Jayne Angel
Art Design	Jayne Angel / Emmesse
Lighting Design	Richard Nicholson
Choregraphy	Ceris Faulkener
Fight Arrangement	Kenan Ali
Soundscape	Dom Bryan
Photography	Paul Tsanos

The Writer:

Catherine Kay is a producer, writer and actress she was born in Manchester (England) in 1973. Catherine studied for a Postgraduate Diploma in Writing for The Stage at the Arden School of Theatre (Manchester) and then diversified her writing for television and film by studying a Masters in Screenwriting at Screen Academy Scotland (Edinburgh). Catherine produced her first play Bubbysaurus 'A play about Love, Friendships, Babies and Raves', in 2004 at Contact Theatre Manchester. In 2005 the Manchester Evening News Theatre Awards nominated Bubbysaurus for Best New Play. Catherine is currently writing an 'inspirational' screenplay set in Newcastle and based on one woman's real life journey from a 'prison cell' to a 'board room'.

Comments on *Just One Day:*

***** **Laura Maley *(The Public Reviews)*:** 'Powerful stuff, well written & intelligently performed – almost required viewing for anyone involved with working with survivors of sexual violence. Kay does not shy away from dealing with any aspect of sexual violence and the script in turn feels unapologetically authentic. It should continue to challenge perceptions of sexual violence and more generally, feminism as well as offering a voice and hope to survivors.'

Porl Cooper (Producer and Theatre Programmer at the Lowry Theatre, Salford): 'I was simultaneously shocked and compelled by this hard hitting powerful script. Catherine's writing is a voice that needs to be heard and hers is an exceptional talent.'

Reba Cohen (Counsellor at Manchester Rape Crisis): 'You can quote me on how much it has helped me understand the experience of the women I counsel.'

(Counsellor at Manchester Rape Crisis): 'Encapsulates the emotional legacy of rape and how it impacts on all relationships.'

(Counsellor at STAR Surviving Trauma after Rape): 'This play will really raise awareness of the impact of on-going emotional, psychological issues rape leaves with a survivor.'

With thanks to:

Porl Cooper Producer & Programmer at the Lowry Theatre (Salford).

Staff & Students at Manchester University Students Union (Manchester).

Staff & Clients at Manchester Rape Crisis the Pankhurst Centre (Manchester).

Staff & Clients at STAR Surviving Trauma after Rape (Wakefield).

Jean Cummings at Crisis, (Scotland).

Baxter Storey based at the Royal Exchange Theatre (Manchester).

Peggy Ramsey Foundation

FOR THE SURVIVORS

Staging and production notes:
The play is set in Manchester (England) 2003. It can be staged End On or in Promenade. There are four main areas of action, Janet and Gary's Flat, The Hospital, The Club/Pub. Any scenes that are set in The Street will take place in the centre of the stage. The set is minimal and consists of four paintings of the central female characters, Shona, Sheldon, Janet and Girl 29. The paintings are to be suspended from the lighting rig with fishing wire.

Characters:
Shona Hurst	Militant Feminist
Janet Sparks	Good Time Girl
Sheldon Lewis	Street Angel
Girl 29	Victim of Drug Rape
Gary Bond	Ex-Soldier
Neil Grimes	Drug Rapist
The Mother	
The Father	
The Boy/Policeman	

ACT ONE SCENE ONE

Girl's night out.
Janet and Gary's flat. Night.
SFX: 'Awful', HOLE.

JANET, enters she is carrying two glasses and her phone. She places the glasses on the table and then checks a text message on her phone

SHELDON and SHONA enter. Sheldon is carrying a bottle of wine. Shona is carrying a carton of cranberry juice

SHELDON (*She hugs Janet*) I ya love. Ah you look nice. Look who's 'ere?

Janet looks unimpressed

SHELDON Shall we 'ave a drink?
JANET   I'll get another glass.
SHONA   I'll pour.

Shona pours three drinks and gives a glass to Janet and a glass to Sheldon

SHELDON (*Glancing out of the window*) Those dirty, pervy workmen are still there? /
JANET   (*She sits down*) They'll be workin' late. /
SHELDON We'll 'ave to walk past 'em on the way to the bussy. /

9

JANET	*(Applying her make up)* I know. I was cringin' the other day when I 'ad to walk past 'em. That fat bald one thinks 'e's fuckin' chocolate. You know what 'e said to the others when I walked by? 'Bride or Bridesmaid'.
SHONA	That's cos you're old.
JANET	I'm not old.
SHELDON	She's as old as Madonna.
JANET	Yeah. No. She's like 43 an' I'm 38. By the way, 'ave I told you I'm engaged? An' 'ave I shown you my ring?
SHONA	Only five times. Let's watch as her spirit and soul slowly slip away into bride land.

Janet shoots Shona a filthy look

SHELDON	It's her spinstercurity. She's Salford paranoid about being left on the shelf.
JANET	I'm not a jar of Christmas pickles.
SHONA	Take her out once a year. /
SHELDON	An' she's anyone's.
SHONA	Don't worry Janet. You're the prettiest. You get all the boys.
JANET	Yeah. You're right. I do. I got the man I wanted. *(She flashes her rock)* Three grand, St Anne's Square.
SHELDON	Ya neva looked up 'ow much 'e paid for it?
JANET	Fuckin right I did.

SHONA	Did you know that Bridesmaids, were originally dressed like the bride to confuse kidnappers who wanted to abduct the bride? Apparently, the groomsmen were warriors who helped the groom fight off the kidnappers. MMmmn. That's a wife for you... Property that's sold to the highest bidder.
JANET	Do ya wanna 'ave a day off?
SHONA	What from?
JANET	Chattin' fuckin' Macca. Anyway listen. I'm walkin' past the workys an' you know what I said when I 'eard 'im? 'Bridesmaid, bridesmaid. Ya fat, old fucker, I wunt touch ya wiv 'is'.

Shona rummages in her bag and pulls out a crumpled skirt
She notices a stain on it

SHELDON	No ya dint.
JANET	I did. Well I dint want them twats finkin I was intimidated by 'em.
SHONA	Is that how you felt? Intimidated?
JANET	Nah. Ya know what men are like? They think they're the funniest fuckers on the planet. So if they're cut dead by a woman in front of their mates. /
SHONA	Total castration.
JANET	Yeah. Summat like that.

SHONA	Is it alright if I borrow a cloth? For this stain?

Shona exits to the kitchen

JANET	In the bowl. No, no, under the sink. I tell ya that fiancé of mine? Since we've started livin' together… Everytime I walk in a room, I've gotta check I'm in me own 'ome. Can't fuckin' find anythin'. 'E's that tidy.
SHONA	Maybe he's adjusting to your biorhythms.
JANET	*(To Sheldon)* Bio fuckin' what? What you doin', invitin' 'er out?
SHELDON	Don't be like that. I felt sorry for 'er. She dunt get out much.
JANET	Neither does Maxine Carr. But we don't invite 'er out of a Saturday night.
SHELDON	Don't speak to me like that.
JANET	Like what?
SHELDON	Like a bitch.
JANET	So I'm a bitch if I speak my mind?
SHELDON	I neva said that. Just sometimes Janet. It's not what you say, it's the way that you say it.
JANET	Yeah, yeah. I've got a bad attitude. Put it on me gravestone when I'm dead. I don't give a fuck.

Sheldon shakes her head in disillusionment

Beat
JANET *(Guiltily)* Come on Shel? You know what I'm sayin'? It's like 'angin' out wiv a traumatised nun. *(Holding up the cranberry juice)* What the fucks that about?

Sheldon smirks

JANET Shall we 'ave another drink?
SHELDON Yeah.
JANET *(Picking up the bottle)* What about a little pick me up for the nun?

She pours some of the wine into Shona's glass

SHELDON No Janet don't. It's tight.
JANET Oh go on. It'll liven 'er up a bit. Put a smile on 'er face.

Shona re-enters wearing a tie dye patterned skirt
Janet hands her a drink

SHELDON Is that what you're wearin'?
SHONA Why?
JANET 'Ow can we put this? Tie dye. It's right up there with the polyester jumper dress in the fashion faux pas stakes.
SHONA Fashion fades. Style remains.
JANET Not in tie die it dunt!

SHELDON	This is not a criticism, but even Kate Moss can't pull off tie dye.
SHONA	Do I look like I give a crap about Kate Moss?
JANET	*(To Sheldon)* She doesn't give a crap about The Queen.
SHELDON	Treachery.
JANET	Off with her 'ead!
SHONA	*(Drinking from her glass)* Are you two going to be like this all night?
JANET	*(Giggling)* Come on Shona, you'd want us./
SHONA	Did you put alcohol in that? /
JANET	To tell ya if you looked like a twa.../
SHONA	*(Spitting out the drink)* YOU BITCH. That's so out of order. *(To Sheldon)* And you. You know I don't drink. /

Janet stifles her laughter

SHONA	I'm glad you find it so funny putting crap in my drink, without my consent.

Shona goes to exit. Janet blocks her from leaving

JANET	Oh come on, Shona. We were only 'avin a laugh. We were just tryin' to get ya in the mood, that's all.
SHONA	In the mood for what?
JANET	A good time.

ACT ONE SCENE TWO

Hospital. Night.
FX: Cross Fade. Lights up on GIRL 29 and THE MOTHER.

*The Mother is wrapping a bandage around Girl 29's arm
She then sits down and speaks to the audience*

MOTHER   After she'd calmed down, she slept solid for near on two days. I'd keep checkin' on 'er to make sure she was alright. 'Er body shook constantly. Lookin' back now, I don't know if that was a reaction to what 'e'd spiked 'er with. After the second day. She come out of the room an' she said, 'Right I've 'ad enough. I'm gonna tell the Police what 'e did to me'. So for the second time Frank took 'er to the station. An' she tried to tell 'em what 'appened./ Well none of it made sense. She cunt remember anythin' in order. Times, dates, places, it was all jumbled. What could they do? They 'ad no other choice. They 'ad to put 'er in this place. It was for 'er own good. Then they sent 'er off to a psychiatrist an' she cried an' cried. 'Tell 'em your fears', I said. 'Tell 'em everythin' that's in your 'ead, tell 'em everythin' that's frightenin' ya'…

ACT ONE SCENE THREE

Janet and Gary's flat. Night.

The Girls are now slightly tipsy and much LOUDER!

SHELDON	So anyway. I'm dancin' away an' I'm feelin' good, an' then outta the blue some guy, behind me, starts gropin' me arse.
JANET	Yeah. An' I clocks this, an' so I say... 'Right Shell, let's swap places'. Sure as eggs is eggs, the cunt starts gropin' me. So I let 'im carry on. Lull 'im into a false sense of security. Let 'im fink I'm gettin' off on what 'e's doin'. An' just as 'e's finkin' that 'e's Don fuckin' Wan. I turn round an' give 'im the 'ardest, loudest most almighty slap.
SHONA	Yeah. But violence just lowers you to their level.
SHELDON	Maybe. But 'e kept 'is fuckin' 'ands to 'imself for the rest of the night.
JANET	Yeah. An' 'is kip looked like 'e'd bin sunbathin' on a slatted deck chair.
SHELDON	Are ya gonna cop off tonight Shona?
SHONA	I don't know.
SHELDON	What 'appened to that lad who asked you out for a drink, but it wunt a date.
SHONA	?

JANET	*(Smirking)* The one who started textin' 'is mate as soon as you arrived.
SHELDON	It's really annoyin' when they do that. Or when they want free therapy over their ex's.
JANET	Well it's like when they say, 'I like the dress you're wearin'. Why can't they just say, 'Can I fuck ya?'
SHONA	There was no mutual attraction.
SHELDON	Can I offer you some advice?
SHONA	?
SHELDON	Men don't like pressure and they don't want to date a political cause.
JANET	She's right. They don't do baggage. Not until they've fallen for ya and seen past your clitoris.
SHONA	Maybe we just didn't fancy each other.
SHELDON	Maybe you dint phone 'im back quick enough, like Janet.

Janet raises her middle finger.

SHELDON	This is not a criticism. But perhaps if you were a little softer. You know / Showed a more vulnerable side.
JANET	Yeah they love all that shit. It makes 'em feel strong and masculine. The truth of the matter is, most men lie to 'emselves. They 'ave too, because deep inside they all think

SHONA	they're worthless sacks of shite. They need us to make 'em feel better about 'emselves. I can't do that sort of thing. It feels wrong. It's insulting and it devalues them.
JANET	Don't ever say that to a man.
SHONA	Why?
JANET	Just don't.
SHELDON	The aim of the game is to make 'im think that 'e's won the ultimate prize. An' that prize is you. Janet lend 'er that book you 'ad.
JANET	What. 'Ow to be a complete bitch an'still make 'im love ya?'
SHELDON	No the other one. What's it called? 'Women Who Love Too Much'. That's it.
SHONA	I've read the sequel.
SHELDON	I dint know it 'ad a follow up.
SHONA	Yeah. 'Men Who Don't Love Enough'.
SHELDON	?
JANET	She's takin' the piss Sheldon.
SHONA	That's such an old fashioned philosophy. Like I said. Property sold to the highest bidder.
JANET	*(Shining her bling)* Well where's your fuckin' finger at night? Excuse me Sheldon. Are you single?
SHELDON	No.
JANET	Excuse me Janet. Are you single? No. Engaged. Excuse me Shona. Are men runnin' for the hills after one date with ya?

SHONA	And there speaks the girl who missed the boat, but got the mansion.
JANET	Look out there. Check out what's on offer. 'Career criminals', 'Lazy doleys' and 'Rat faced youths'. I've got a good man an e's got a good job an' I'm gonna keep 'old of 'im.
SHELDON	You forgot middle aged baldys.
JANET	?
SHELDON	I'm quite 'appy with mine.
JANET	*(Sneering)* There's more to life than bein' single.

ACT ONE SCENE FOUR

Hospital. Day.
SFX: 'Miss World', HOLE.
FX: Lights up on Girl 29 and Shona.

This scene has taken place a couple of days earlier. (Pre girl's night out.)
Shona is sitting on a chair.
Girl 29 doesn't acknowledge Shona. She is sewing on a large piece of cloth.

SHONA	Protect yourself. Ask for male Police officers to deal with your case. They'll treat you better, and we need to show them the damage that their gender leaves behind. Always ask for a female doctor and tell the psychiatrists nothing.
Beat	
	I didn't like it when the psychiatrist asked me questions. I don't have any hang ups about my childhood. I was loved and cared for. I had a good relationship with my father. That's relationship. Not sexual relationship. 'It's not me who should be answering these questions'. I said. 'This is bullshit'.

Beat
Shona takes her embroidery from her bag and starts to sew.

Pause
I didn't think that you'd want to talk so I bought mine. A woman's work is never done.

No matter how dirty you feel. The skin always sheds itself.

Girl 29 stares blankly at Shona, and then continues sewing.

ACT ONE SCENE FIVE

Night.
FX: Spotlight on GARY.

He's sitting on a chair smoking a fag. He speaks to the audience.

GARY I know 'er from off the estate. I was lookin' out for 'er. She was 'alf cut an' some pricks were givin' 'er shit in the pub. I 'elped 'er outside into a taxi. I thought that was the right thing to do. To be honest she was pawin' at me, wunt let go a me. Me fiancé wunt 'ave bin 'appy wiv that. Ya know what a mean.

ACT ONE SCENE SIX

Pub. Night.
FX: Spotlight on the FATHER.

He's sitting on a chair and supping his pint.

FATHER She was two years old when I met 'er mother. I always thought of 'er as me own. I changed 'er nappies, took 'er to nursery. She was a very bright child. Always thought she'd do big things with 'er life. *(Silence)* When she first turned up on the doorstep an' told me, I dint know what she was sayin'. 'There was a man', she said. "E 'elped me into a taxi an then I don't remember anythin'. 'I think 'e did somethin', did somethin' bad to me', she said. That's all she kept sayin', over and over. Margaret, she said, 'Frank. Phone the police. There's somethin' not right'. But God forgive me. I just thought I can't. You just. / Don't want to think anythin' like. / I don't wanna think it's true. Things like that don't 'appen to ordinary decent people.

Lights fade

ACT ONE SCENE SEVEN

Janet and Gary's flat. Night.
FX: Lights up on the Girls.

Janet is sitting on a chair. Sheldon is straightening Janet's hair with straighteners.
Shona is sat on the floor looking through cds.

SHELDON   That's a point. Where 'ave all the flashers gone? You don't see any of 'em anymore.
JANET   Probably sick of us lot laughin' at 'em. I wunt mind they've always got a cock the size of a peanut.
SHONA   I read in one of my course text books, that if a man flashes at a woman when she's alone in an isolated public place, the first thing she thinks of is imminent death and the second thing she thinks of is rape.
JANET   Oh god, did you 'ear about Tanya?
SHELDON   Margaret's Tanya? /
JANET   Yeah 'er. The other day Margaret broke down at work an' started blubbin', goin' on about Tanya an' 'ow she's lost it. She thinks she was raped. I mean I think, you'd know if you'd bin raped or not. /
SHELDON   Margaret must be gutted. *(Pause)* I bet that's why she's finished up at work an' signed on the sick.
JANET   'Ow can ya not know if you've bin raped?

SHONA	She was drugged.
SHELDON	'Ow do you know?
SHONA	I went to see her last week.
SHELDON	Is she ok?
SHONA	No.
JANET	I bet the dozy bint went 'ome with some psycho.
SHELDON	Janet!
SHONA	Margaret said that some guy helped her into a taxi and then she doesn't remember anythin' after that.
JANET	Yeah you see. She copped with some psycho. If you go 'ome wiv a stranger, you're takin' a risk aren't ya?
SHELDON	Yeah, well, we don't know all the facts do we. What are women supposed to do? Never talk to men or go out alone at night. An' that's really 'arsh. How would you feel if it 'appened to you?
JANET	Oh please. Do ya fink any man wud chance 'is cock, tryin' to rape me?
SHONA	I don't think it works like that.
JANET	All I'm sayin' is, don't take the short cut through the graveyard. Spare yourself unnecessary risks.
SHELDON	Sometimes Janet you're such a dick.

Silence

SHONA	One of the women on my course told me that she was living in Bradford at the time of the Yorkshire Ripper murders. One night she was walking home and she got stopped by the police. /
SHELDON	What for?
SHONA	They wanted to give her a lift home.
JANET	Nice. The amount of times I've tried to cadge a lift 'ome from them fuckers when I've bin pissed, an' they've refused.
SHONA	The point I'm making, is that when they'd dropped her home and she was getting out of the car, she asked them if they were stopping all the men out on the street and giving them a lift home.
SHELDON	What did they say?
SHONA	No.
JANET	But surely, if there were men out, they'd be more likely to stop them?
SHELDON	*(Looking out of the window)* Why dint they give the men a lift 'ome?
SHONA	I don't know.
JANET	*(Smirking)* Maybe that was their way of keepin' the streets safe.
SHONA	Maybe.
SHELDON	Those dirty, pervy bastards are still out there. We'll 'ave to walk past 'em on the way ta the bussy.

FX: CROSS FADE.

Lights up on Gary sat in the pub.

GARY It's all paranoia in 'er 'ead. Typical bird in it. Can't 'andle 'er drugs. I mean, whatever she's sayin' mate, it wunt me. I fink you're best off tryin' to find the driver of the taxi. I dint fink to check cos some of 'em are proper dodgy. She just got in the cab an' give the guy 'er address. An' then I went back 'ome to me Mrs mate. That's all I can tell ya. I mean anythin' else she's sayin' is bollocks.

ACT ONE SCENE EIGHT

Street. Night.
SFX: 'Entertain', SLEATER KINNEY.
SFX: Rain and crowd /traffic noises, to depict a busy street in the centre of Manchester on a Saturday night.
FX: Light change.

Janet, Sheldon and Shona leave the flat and cut through the centre of the audience.

JANET	Pissin' rain. Me 'airs gonna look a state.
SHELDON	Janet I need to talk to you. /
JANET	Not now Shel. *(She starts to run)* I need to get me 'air outta this rain. /
SHELDON	It's serious Janet.
JANET	So's this. You know 'ow long it takes me to straighten me Lego 'air. Then the fuckin' Manchester weather goes an' pisses on it.

The Girls exit

SFX: Music Fades
FX: Light change

The Father stands alone in the street
Beat

FATHER I see some of these girls, out an' about, 'alf undressed an' I fear for 'em I do. Rape's not a fair fight, but with that stuff, they don't stand a chance. I looked it up on the internet. They call it roofies. Makes it sound 'armless like takin' toffees. *(Pause)* It wipes a person's memory. Can make 'em do crazy things. I know my girl would neva take anythin' like that. Yeah, she likes a drink. Like any kid. But that. *(Pause)* The coppers said it was difficult to get evidence when a girls bin drug raped. They said there's not been any proven cases of rohyhpnol bein' used. They told me it disappears from a girl's body within 4 to 6 hours. Vanishes in Just One Day. It's not just rohyhpnol they use either. They can get these over-the-counter drugs that make you drowsy if you take 'em wiv alcohol. He told me they get over 30 cases a week in The Royal. More at the weekend. Girls turnin' up at A&E confused an' not knowin' what's 'appened to 'em. *(Pause)* I know I shunt. But I just. / I just keep seein' 'er lyin' there. / Not bein' able to move. *(Pause)* What terrors she must be seein'.

The Father exits

ACT ONE SCENE NINE

Club. Night.
SFX: 'Celebrity Skin', HOLE. / 'Debaser', THE PIXIES.
FX: Light change.

Janet and Sheldon enter the club and walk directly to the bar. They deliberately leave Shona prizing her way through the audience.

Sheldon takes 4 vodka shots from THE BARMAN and hands him a tenner.

SFX: Fade Music.

JANET	She's gettin' right on my tits. Makin' fuckin' snide comments. 'I missed the boat, but got the mansion?' Is she takin' the piss, cos I live in a council 'ouse?
SHELDON	I know you think she's turned into a nark, but she's alright. /
JANET	If I 'ear men are this. Men are that. Conspiracy theory this. One more time. Why can't she just be a woman an' be 'appy about it?
SHELDON	Janet. You know last Saturday? /
JANET	She's never bin right since she did that stint in Scary Marys. Dint they section 'er for bein' a danger to 'erself?

SHELDON   I don't know. / You know last Saturday was Gary out in Summervilles? /
JANET   What?

The Barman approaches Janet and Sheldon

JANET   Oh, 'ere we go...
BARMAN   Are you 'avin' a good night?
JANET   *(Surly)* I was.
BARMAN   Nice dress.
JANET   *(Snapping)* Look. I'm gonna be really direct with ya, ok. Ya not fit enough. You dress like a tramp an' we're taken.
BARMAN   *(Walks away)* Fuckin' ugly, old bitch. (Janet loses it and grabs him)
JANET   An' ugly, old bitch, you were gonna shag a few seconds ago.
SHELDON   *(Pulling her off him)* Janet.
BARMAN   Crazy slag.

Janet composes herself and glances around, slightly paranoid about her outburst

SHELDON   What was that about?
JANET   Why should I deny my instinct of self-protection?
SHELDON   *(Beat)* Because you weren't under attack. Because that gimp over there will chuck us out and that twat over there will end up 'avin a better night than us.

JANET	CUNTS. (*Janet's mobile vibrates and she pulls it out from her bag*) Fuckin Gary again. Three missed calls it's like 'avin me very own stalker. We're not even married yet.

She puts the mobile back in her bag.

SHELDON	Listen Janet. I wasn't gonna say anythin' because of your engagement an' that. But I saw Gary out last Saturday an' 'e was chattin to another girl.
JANET	So. 'E can chat to other girls. I don't fuckin' own 'im. An' besides 'e was wiv me last Saturday night, so you've got your wires crossed.
SHELDON	It definitely looked like 'im.
JANET	Obviously not, cos 'e was wiv me all night. What is it that she's studying at college?
SHELDON	*(Beat)* Women's studies.
JANET	You know, my old ma used to say, 'Women who strive to be equal to men, lack ambition'.
SHELDON	Yeah. Ya neva see a man strivin' to be equal to a woman do ya?
JANET	I spose braggin' about the size of your period isn't as interestin' as 'im braggin' about the size of 'is cock.
SHELDON	Women's studies it's a bit 1980's in it? / This is dead tight but have you 'eard 'ow

	she's started talkin' on the phones at work? *(Mimicking Shona)* Like this, like that. You know, that posh voice to make 'er sound more intelligent.
JANET	Yeah. I know. It's fuckin' embarrassin'. It's a shitty mcjob in a call centre. Like anyone gives a shit? You know, sometimes, if a customer gets on me tits at work, I put 'em through to 'er extension.
SHELDON	God I thought I was the only one that did that. I put 'em through to my Tommy's mobile when 'e's pissin' me off. *(Both girls laugh in unison)* That fuckin' skirt.
JANET	I know. My Gary calls 'er the kiss of death. She scares the shit out of 'im.
SHELDON	What does 'e say about me be 'ind my back?
JANET	Fuckin' all sorts.
SHELDON	Charmin'.
JANET	Don't take it personally. 'E's a man. 'E wants me all to 'imself.

Her mobile vibrates. She takes it out of her bag again

JANET	It's fuckin' 'im again. I'm not goin' 'ome. That's what 'e wants. *(Speaking into the phone)* What d'ya want? *(She covers her other ear)* You're gonna 'ave to speak up. I can't 'ear ya. / 'Ang on, I'll take it outside.

She signals to Sheldon that she is going to take the call outside

Janet exits

ACT ONE SCENE TEN

Hospital. Night.

FX: Lights up on The Mother and Girl 29.

The Mother is sitting on a chair. Girl 29 is drawing

MOTHER   She's always liked makin' things. Paintin', drawin', puttin' things together. I used to say, 'Oh all that 'arty farty stuff, what d ya get outta that'? 'I like it', she'd say. 'It makes me 'appy'. When she was two she wunt speak. I took 'er to the doctors cos I thought she want developin' properly. 'There's nowt wrong with 'er', 'e said. I told me mother. 'She dunt talk', I said.
'Yes, I know', said me mother.
'But she's very musical'.
'Musical', I said.
'Well that's no bloody use. I want 'er to speak'.
Now look at 'er. She's just the same. Sat there silent. An' all she does is bloody sew an' draw. Day in an' day out.

ACT ONE SCENE ELEVEN

Street. Night.

Shona and Sheldon walk through the audience. They are sharing a tray of chips

Janet walks behind them. She is texting on her mobile

SHONA   Apparently a survey was done in the Northwest with young males and a third of them admitted that when their girlfriends were drunk, they took sexual advantage of them.

SHELDON   Yeah. But I do that. When my Tommy comes 'ome an' 'e's 'ad a skin full. I love to bend 'im in all shapes an' sizes. 'E's more pliable.

SHONA   What's disturbing about that is the idea that young men think that sex is something that you do to a woman and not with a woman.

SHELDON   Oh lighten up Shona. There's no need to criminalise the yoot. You'll be slappin' an ASBO on them next for lookin' at a girls arse.

SHONA   I don't know. Is sexual behaviour becoming more experimental or more misogynistic? Do you know that the two most favourite sexual turn ons for men are

	'coming in a woman's face' and 'shagging a woman up the arse'.
SHELDON	Nice. Tommy tried the up-the-arse thing wiv me once. So I pulled out my old 'strap on' from the side drawer and said 'You first?' 'E dint ask again.
SHONA	Do you think it's a homo erotic thing?
SHELDON	No. It's just tighter on their cock and my fanny takes offence at that.
SHONA	The other day I found out that the women who are most at risk of being drug raped are women aged 30 to 50 years old.
SHELDON	So they rape 'old birds' too?
SHONA	More so than the youngsters. Perhaps they think 'old birds' are more erotic, or up for a good rapin'.
SHELDON	Either that, or they think we're desperate. Who's doin' it? Who are they?
SHONA	I've got this theory that it's. /
SHELDON	/Sad, slimy, sexually inadequate middle aged men.
SHONA	Or just someone's best mate. And the worst of it is, for most of the drug rape victims, they don't know whose raped them. Imagine that. Every time a man walks passed you on the street, serves you in a corner shop, sits behind you on a bus, you think the same thought to yourself. He could have raped me.
SHELDON	God it makes you hate them.

Janet stops texting and looks at Shona.

JANET   FOR FUCKS SAKE. WILL YOU SHUT THE FUCK UP.
SHELDON   Janet!
JANET   I'm sick of 'er. If you don't wanna drink. If you wanna spout off about women's rights. Fine. Do it. But don't fuckin' ram it down our throats.

Pause

SHELDON   Janet. What's the matter?

Beat

JANET   Gary. Yesterday that little slut Tanya 'Udson, made an allegation of rape against 'im. She said./ She remembers him 'elpin' 'er into a taxi the night she was raped.
SHELDON   When.
JANET   What?
SHELDON   When? What night was she raped?
JANET   I don't know. Last Saturday. Does it matter? She was obviously pissed or off 'er 'ead on fuckin' ketamine or somethin'.
SHELDON   Are you sure he was with you Janet?
JANET   I can't believe you're even asking me that. It's a lie. She's a fuckin' lyin' little bitch an' she's not gonna get away with it.

The Girls exit.

ACT TWO SCENE ONE

NEIL is seated amongst the audience. He stands up and walks centre stage.

FX: Single spotlight on Neil.
THE BEAST REARS HIS HEAD
SFX: 'Rape Me', NIRVANA.

NEIL Every Satday, I clean the whore bus, ready for cruisin' on a Sunday. / Birds me own age. / They think they're better than me. / With young pussy I don't 'ave to ask pretty fuckin' please for sex. *(Beat)* A couple of weeks ago I picked up two girls about 12 years old. / Held a knife to one of the whores throats an' got them both in the van. / They were squealin' like little pigs. *(Mimicking)* 'We're too young, we're too young' / SHUT THE FUCK UP. / I picked 'em up an' flung 'em on the mattress. / I got the knife an' slid it down Whore 1's t-shirt. / It sliced the cotton in two an' fell away, like silk, exposin' 'er little tits. / She was just sproutin'. / They were 'ard. Like little bulbs. / I told the other to suck me off but she just sat there like a fuckin' retard. / So I slammed 'er 'ead down on me cock an' she started noshin'. *(Beat)* While she was noshin' me I

asked the other one if 'er boyfriends cock was as nice as mine. / Tears started streamin' down 'er face, an' she kept sayin' 'we don't 'ave boyfriends, we don't 'ave boyfriends'. /
(Beat) Well I said. / SSsshh. / 'I'm just teachin' a little lesson for when you do'.
(Beat) I can't remember shootin' me load. / After I'd dumped 'em both in a ditch. / I looked at me watch an' only 10 minutes 'ad passed. / It was all over an' done wiv like a flash. / I thought afterwards. I could 'ave kept 'em longer. / *(Pause)* /When I got 'ome, I 'ad to clean the fuckin' van again. It stank a fuckin' piss.

Neil exits.

Lights fade.

ACT TWO SCENE TWO

Janet and Gary's flat. Day.
FX: Lights up on Janet and Gary's flat.
SFX: 'Asking For It' HOLE.

Gary is sitting on the couch watching the television.

Janet is standing and smoking a cigarette. She is looking intensely into the distance.

GARY	What's up?
JANET	*(Stubbing out the cigarette)* Fuckin' nothin'.
GARY	'As someone said sommat?

She picks up a magazine that has been stashed behind the couch and opens it up at a 'split beaver' shot. (The audience see this)

JANET   Doreen from Doncaster. 'I just can't 'elp it. My clothes are always fallin' off me an' my tits come spillin' out.' Yeah. I know what she means. I 'ave that problem all the fuckin' time. Especially in Tesco. *(Beat)* Is there somethin' wrong with my tits? If there is, you know what you can do? Fuck off an' fuck someone else.

GARY   It's just a bit a porn that's all.
JANET   Is it?

GARY   It dunt make me think any differently about ya.
JANET   You cunt 'ave thought that fuckin' much about me in the first place to be wankin' over this shit.
GARY   It's a laugh that's all. Me an' the the lads read it sometimes.

Janet chucks the porn mag at him and hundreds of dismembered images of naked female bodies spray out onto the floor and over the audience

JANET   Do you an' the lad's rape women an' all?
GARY   What?
JANET   You 'eard.

Pause

JANET   Did you rape that girl?
GARY   No.
JANET   Did you rape that girl?
GARY   No, no. I wunt do nothin' like that. You've got ta believe me Janet.

Long Pause

JANET   If I've lied to the coppers to save the skin of a rapist, you'll 'ave more than a stretch inside to worry about.

GARY   I told ya. We got in a fight wiv a couple of other lads. You know what Neil's like when 'e's 'ad a few. If they pull me in they'll come down on me like a ton of shit cos I've got previous an' I'm ex-army.

Beat

JANET   Sheldon said she seen you with some girl, outside Summervilles. Was it 'er?
GARY   Janet. I wasn't wiv any girl. I told ya. We went out for lasts. Got into a bit of a scuffle on the way 'ome and then crashed at Neil's after. End of.

Pause

              Do you remember what I said when we first met?

Beat

JANET   You said, you dint know what a girl like me could see in a boy like you.
GARY   You were everythin' to me. You still are.
JANET   Don't fuck wiv my ead Gary.
GARY   I'm not. I swear. I wunt do that. I dint rape 'er. I neva raped any girl. You've got ta believe me.
JANET   If you didn't do it. You've got nothin' to worry about.

Pause

GARY   Is this how it's always gonna be?
JANET   ?
GARY   We've bin together for 18 months, an' ya still don't trust me.
JANET   Trust is earned.
GARY   What about love?
JANET   *(Snapping)* I'm with ya aren't I?
GARY   Are ya? 18 months / an' ya still can't say the words.
JANET   ?
GARY   Do ya fink it's some kind of weakness to admit ya love me. / Or do ya fink I'm gonna lock you up in a cage once you've said it.
JANET   *(Screaming)* I FUCKIN LOVE YA. / Alright

Pause

GARY   That's not quite 'ow I imagined the moment.
JANET   I said it. You made me say it before I was ready.
GARY   You know your problem Janet? You're too stubborn. 'My way or the highway.' You've gotta a fuckin' war goin' on inside ya self all the time. Ya don't know whether to love me or hate me. Which

Beat

                  Janet am I gonna wake up wiv tommorra? The Janet that loves me? The Janet that'll slot me in 'er life for the day? Or the Janet that wants to annihilate me? Everythins' black an' white wiv ya. There's no fuckin' room for negotiation.

                  I love ya. I wanna be your 'usband. I chose you.

Beat

                  You can keep on pushin' me away. But every time I'll expose ya. I'll expose ya tricks. An' what will you be left with Janet? What will you be left with?

JANET   Finished? An' you know your problem? You can't give a straight answer to a straight question. An' it pisses me off.

GARY   I answered your question.

Beat

                  Don't bail on me Janet. I need you.

JANET   If you dint do it, you've got nowt to worry about.

SFX: *'Asking For It' 2, HOLE.*

Gary exits. Janet positions herself on the couch and reads her wedding magazine

ACT TWO SCENE THREE

Hospital. Day.
FX: Single spots on Girl 29, Shona and The Mother.

Girl 29 is sitting on a chair and sewing. Shona is sitting at the right hand side of her. The Mother is sitting at the left hand side of Shona

SHONA   I used to think everyone knew. That everyone could see inside me. But they can't. People don't know anything about you, unless you tell them. But these places are the biggest shame. You're totally powerless in here.

Beat

When my brother collected me from the hospital he told me that we were going out for a drink with his friends. He told me not to talk about being raped to his friends. 'Why', I said?

Beat

The nights were the worst thing. Every noise in the house I'd be up. Standing at the top of the stairs. Checking cupboards, peeping out of curtains. There was one night, two months after it happened. I felt myself drifting off to sleep and there he was. / His face. / Really quickly, it flashed into my thoughts. Then he was gone. It was like someone flicking a light switch on and off in my head. I know it's still up there what he did to me. I never stop wondering what he did to me. One time a friend, if you can call them that. / Said to me, 'At least you were drugged and you don't know what happened.' But that's just it. /

Beat

Not knowing. It's worse than knowing.

ACT TWO SCENE FOUR

Hospital. Day.

MOTHER	I said some terrible things.
SHONA	I'm sure you didn't mean them. We've all missed you at work.
MOTHER	I'm not goin' back there. 'Avin' Janet Sparks, sneerin' at me. I accused Tanya of bein' a fantasist. Told 'er she'd bought shame on the family. 'Who'd rape you?' I said.
SHONA	You were in shock. The mind handles stress in different ways.
MOTHER	It upsets me. Seein' 'er in 'ere. It's, it's like a prison.

Sheldon enters

SHELDON	'Ow is she?
SHONA	Fine.
SHELDON	Did you get 'er to wash?
SHONA	She won't do that. I'm going to get some drinks.
SHELDON	'Ow long 'ave you bin comin' 'ere for counselling?
SHONA	For three years on and off. I still need the odd session now and again. *(She smirks)* For when I'm feeling really mental. That's how I found out about Tanya.

Pause

SHELDON   I saw 'im with 'er. Gary. /
SHONA   When? /
SHELDON   On the night she was raped. I was with the Street Angels. *(Sheldon pulls out a bottle stopper from her bag)*
SHELDON   We 'and these out in the clubs. They protect drinks from bein' spiked. /
SHONA   When? /
SHELDON   You just put 'em in the top of your bottle.
SHONA   What did you see? /
SHELDON   They were invented by a man, after 'is daughter was drug raped. /
SHONA   What did you see?

Pause

SHELDON   He 'elped 'er in a taxi. She cud hardly stand up. Then 'e got in the taxi wiv 'er, an' it drove off towards the estate.
SHONA   Why didn't you stop him?
SHELDON   I thought 'e was 'elpin' 'er, an' I wasn't sure if it was Tanya. I just saw the back of 'er. But it was definitely Gary.
SHONA   Gary's a rapist.
SHELDON   You don't know that.
SHONA   I do. I can spot a rapist at a 50 mile radius.
SHELDON   That's exactly why I've not said anythin'. We can't just jump to conclusions.

SHONA · You've got to tell the police.
SHELDON · There's fuck all they can do. You shud know that.
SHONA · If you don't tell them I will.
SHELDON · Janet's not gonna appreciate you twistin' the knife.
SHONA · As long as women are being raped, I'll always twist the knife.
SHELDON · Tut. It's like belongin' to some club for you.

Silence

I was sexually assaulted once. Some little shit in the swimmin' baths. He thought it'd be funny to stick 'is hand up me crotch while I was swimmin'. I was with my Tommy, 'e was playin' in the pool wiv our Gemma. I neva told 'im, cos I knew 'e'd go nuts an' the little prick was wiv a load of lads. I dint want Tommy to get 'urt. For weeks after, every time Tommy touched me down there I felt that little shits 'and.

Beat

But that's what the little prick wanted. I dint want to give 'im the satisfaction of 'urtin' me boyfriend as well.

Sheldon and Shona exit
Lights Fade

ACT TWO SCENE FIVE

Shona alone. Night.
FX: Light change.
SFX: 'Doll Parts' 1, HOLE.

Shona walks centre stage
She is holding a box full of old photographs The box reads, 'I Love Boys'. She slowly hands out the photographs to the audience

SHONA   People always treat you differently when they know. With some you see the pity in their eyes, others the horror. Some feel obliged to protect you. Some want to apologise. Some want to understand you. Some despise you, some even try to love you. / Then there's the ones who want to take away the pain. The succession of therapists, teaching you coping strategies. Asking you to take responsibility for your actions. Making you aware that no person is 'defined by sexual assault' or 'suffering'. It's difficult not to feel 'defined' when your psyche's been colonised by male hatred. And your body's been infected by sexual violence. It's not that I don't think I deserve to be loved. It's just the threat of intimacy creeps me out. Succumbing to a lover's mouth a lover's hand, a lover's

Beat

love. Even if I can't control anything else in the world I want to know I can control my body.

I hate becoming a drain or a burden on another person. Co-dependency's such a drag. Nobody loves somebody who needs all the time. Men are scared away by the rawness of pure human need.

Beat

It's hard for it not to become an issue in relationships. You're always having to consider how it will make the other person feel. If you tell them or choose not to tell them. Why you feel compelled to scrub their cum off your body, after you've had sex with them. Why you have an aversion to blowjobs, or commitment. How they'll feel if any of 'your issues' should arise at an untimely moment. You don't want to stigmatise or sully yourself with unnecessary weakness. You suddenly become responsible for their reactions as well as learning how to deal with your own.

Beat

It's a lot to ask of someone. So sometimes it's just easier to go for a one night stand.

She exits

SFX: PLAY OUT WITH 'Doll Parts' 2, HOLE.
FX: Lights Fade.

ACT TWO SCENE SIX

Night.
Janet alone.
Mrs. Ogyny, coming atcha.

SFX: 'Sheela-Na-Gig', PJ HARVEY.

FX: Janet enters, (like Queen Cleopatra); she is carried by The Father, Gary, Neil and The Barman.

*She is lowered to her feet by the men and she walks centre stage
Music fades out*

JANET   Girls, girls, girls with your trickery, your frippery and your feminine fiction. You're bitches. Devious bitches. You plot and scheme and keep your anger and disgust buried deep inside because you haven't got the balls to spit it out in the face of society. You're not to be trusted. You say no. You mean yes. You say maybe, you mean 'Only if he buys me enough drinks and pays my taxi 'ome'. You pimp your personalities and offer up your victim credentials, as if they were designer goods. Like an unruly teenager you wield your sexual power to bait your prey. And then when you're faced with the prospect of hard cock you hold off with your token resistance. Heaven help that man if he

	never phones you back. You whinge and whine to your girlfriends about how all men are disappointing shits and how he was nothing more than a user, a non-committal twat and a rapist. You want equality? Then women and children, LAST OFF THE BOAT! Are you helpless? Are you so conditioned by guilt and society's bullshit that you can't take responsibility for your own actions? Do you need a label to work out who you are? Or just a slogan to validate your opinions?
JANET	*(She mimics helplessness to Gary)* 'Oh I was pissed. I thought I wanted it. Then I realised I just didn't fancy 'im that much'. *(To Neil)* 'Oh, I like it rough, I have a secret rape fantasy, but that was just a little too realistic'. *(To the audience)* 'The date just didn't go as planned. I wanted the other guy but ended up with my best mate's boyfriend'. 'Don't tell 'er, she'll think I'm a desperate, dirty, old slag'.
Beat	
	When will you learn, you silly girls? You're not to be trusted.

She pulls out a pink revolver from her pants and aims it at the audience. She pulls the trigger.

SFX: Of 6 gun shots.

ACT TWO SCENE SEVEN

Janet and Gary's flat. Night.
Janet and Gary's engagement party.
SFX: 'She's Lost Control', JOY DIVISION.

Sheldon dances through the centre of the audience
Janet is sitting on Gary's lap. He is smoking a joint
Neil is drinking a bottle of Pils and watching Sheldon dance
Shona is watching Neil

JANET   Neil do your Hooky.
NEIL   Fuck off.
JANET   Go on, you sly bastard. It's funny as fuck.

Neil imitates Peter Hook. He skids across a pretend stage with a pretend bass in his hands

JANET   Cracks me up.

SFX: Fade music low.

Neil launches into a verbal impression of Hooky

NEIL   So I said to the fuckin' Tax man. 'What ya talkin' about? / t-shirts, t-shirts. I aint sold no fuckin' t-shirts. We don't do merchandise at our gigs'. So 'e said, 'Well 'ow come I seen 'alf a Salford wearin' 'em then?' 'So you know what? I just branded a fuckin' ipod instead. 'GET ME ON THAT ONE CUNT'.

(Gary and Janet in unison)
Manchester. It's the love that can't shut up about itself.

GARY   *(dragging on his draw)* I wunt know, I'm Salfordian.
JANET   Yeah. We're its piss pot poor, ugly sista.
GARY   It's feral son.
SHONA   The police have just pulled up outside.

Neil walks to the window. Janet follows him

NEIL   What the fuck do those cunts want?
JANET   I'm not 'avin this.

She exits to answer the door

GARY   Janet. Watch your trap.
JANET   What?
GARY   Don't go in there guns blazin' cos it'll get their backs up.
JANET   Let me 'andle this Gary.
NEIL   Fucks sake.

Neil exits via the backdoor
Janet opens the front door

JANET   Good evenin' officer. What can I do for ya.
POLICEMAN   Does a Mr Gary Bond live 'ere?

JANET   Yes 'e does. 'E's me fiancé. /
POLICEMAN   I'm sorry love. I'm gonna 'ave to come in./

The copper enters the flat

JANET   This is a private party to celebrate our engagement. /
POLICEMAN   We've bin issued with a warrant for 'is arrest. /

Janet follows the copper

JANET   Gate crashers not welcome. / What ya arrestin' 'im for? 'E's 'elped ya with your enquiries. An' I already told ya. He was wiv me the night that bitch was raped.
GARY   It's ok Janet. /
POLICEMAN   Mr Bond. /
JANET   No it's not okay. This Fucker can't just come bargin' in my 'ouse an' arrest my boyfriend for rape. Ya can't do this 'e's got rights.
POLICEMAN   I know. /

The copper reads him his rights and cuffs him

JANET   Ah come on. This is a wind up. It's me engagement party.
SHELDON   It's alright Janet.

58

Sheldon consoles Janet

JANET   I don't fuckin' believe this. 'E's done nothin' wrong. It's lies all of it. It's all lies. Why's she doin' this to us?

Music Fades
Lights fade

ACT TWO SCENE EIGHT

Pub. Night.
FX: Single spotlight on The Father.

The Father is sitting on a chair drinking his pint

FATHER I remember when she got 'er first proper boyfriend. She was 16 an' she'd just started 'er A-levels. They were goin' to a college do an' 'e'd come to collect 'er. That day Margaret 'ad bin cleanin' 'er room an' 'ad found an' open packet of condoms in 'er side drawer. Well, I went ballistic. 'What's she got them for?' I said. 'I wud 'ave thought that was obvious'. Said Margaret. 'Well I'm not 'appy about it'. I said. 'At least she's bloody usin' 'em', said Margaret. Anyway 'e knocked on around 9. 'E 'ad a suit on, 'alf caste from Wythenshawe. She cunt 'alf pick 'em. I remember grabbin' 'is tie an' sayin', 'I want 'er 'ome by 12. Do you 'ear me lad?' 'Yes Mr 'Udson', 'e said. 'No problem Mr 'Udson', 'e said. 'Right', I said. 'Don't you be takin' the piss'.

Beat

I always said that I'd be the one to give 'er away at 'er weddin'. But after it 'appened

Beat

she said she dint want to get married. She said. /

She said. / She never wanted to look at another man again. I shud 'ave bin there to protect 'er.

Beat

I 'OPE THEY LOCK THAT BASTARD UP AN' THROW AWAY THE KEY. 'E DESERVES TO ROT IN HELL FOR WHAT 'E DID.

Light Fades

ACT TWO SCENE NINE

Janet and Gary's flat. Night.
FX: Lights up.

Janet it sat on the couch. Shona is sat on a chair next to her.
Janet snaps her phone shut
Sheldon enters from the kitchen and gives Janet a brew

JANET	They've charged 'im. They said that a witness saw 'im wiv Tanya.

Sheldon glances nervously at Shona

	On the night she was raped. Gettin' into a taxi.
SHONA	It was me.
JANET	Eh?
SHONA	He was seen with Tanya.
JANET	What?
SHONA	On the night of the rape. He got into a cab with her.

Beat

JANET	It was you?
SHONA	It was me who called the police, but not me who saw him.
JANET	Why are you sayin' this Shona?
SHONA	Because it's the truth.
JANET	No. It's not the truth. You're not right. You've never been right since. /

SHONA	Since what? I was raped. /
JANET	Well, we don't know that, do we?
SHONA	I know it.
JANET	What did 'e ever do to you? You're sposed to be my friend.
SHONA	He's a rapist.

Janet bolts off the couch and goes for her throat
Sheldon stands in between them both

SHELDON	Janet. / Don't 'it 'er. / It was me. / It was me. / I saw 'im. / I told 'er not to say anythin'. I knew this would 'appen. It was 'im. I cunt see the woman 'e was with. / But I definitely saw him about 11ish, outside Summervilles.

Janet pulls away from Sheldon's grip and turns away from both girls
Silence

JANET	They're all the enemy, aren't they? Don't ever think that just because I don't read books on women's rights that I don't know 'ow some women think.
SHONA	I've never thought that you're stupid Janet.
JANET	You look down on me like I'm a fuckin' hostage because I choose to share my life with a man. "BRIDELAND." / "SHE

	MISSED THE BOAT." / You resent my 'appiness, because you're a fucked up human bein'.
SHONA	Yeah. You're right. I am fucked up. And yes. It was the fucked up actions of a man that fucked me up. But I'd never use that as a reason to fuck up somebody else's life. Why would I do that?
JANET	So that we can all side with you in your great hate men campaign. Those 'orrible men. / Letchin', leerin' an' rapin'. Because then you can always be the fuckin' VICTIM that you so bravely make out you're not. /
SHONA	I'M NOT A VICTIM. I'M NOT A VICTIM.
JANET	You were raped. It was shitty. Get over it.
SHONA	Don't ever call me a victim.

Pause

JANET	Then don't shit on my life an' think you can get away with it.

SFX: 'Dying', HOLE
Shona and Sheldon exit. Janet exits
Lights Fade

ACT TWO SCENE TEN

Pub. Day.
FX: Lights up.

Gary and Neil are sat at a table in a quiet corner of the pub

NEIL	I can't explain the feelins. / My 'eart starts poundin'. / I get a weird feelin' in the pit of me stomach. /
GARY	/What if stuff starts comin' back to 'er? /
NEIL	/I don't get an' 'ard on. / I just get the desire to 'ave a woman.
GARY	We shunt 'ave done it. /
NEIL	The fantasy's get stronger an' stronger. /
GARY	It got out of 'and. /
NEIL	*(Chilling and controlling. Beat)* Seen your Janet yesterday. She goes in that pie shop on Oxford Road for 'er dinner. Sometimes she alternates an' goes for a chinky in China Town.

Beat

She's never bin my type. / Always 'ad that... / Whiff o' chav about 'er. I spose if I was really desperate I cud put a bag over 'er 'ead.

Neil takes a photograph out of his pocket and throws it on the table. The photo is of Gary with Girl 29

	If you're asked anythin' else you reply no comment, no comment. Right.
GARY	Right.

Gary picks up the photograph and puts it in his coat pocket
Gary exits. Neil walks centre stage
FX: Lights up on Neil

NEIL	One night I followed some bird. / Followed 'er through the subway. / It was late. / There was no one about./ I cud see she was shittin' 'erself. / Just before she cut round the corner, she stopped. / Turned an' walked towards me. / *(Mimicking her)* 'I hope you don't mind'. She said. 'But it's late an' I'm feeling a little scared about walking home on my own. / Would you walk with me'?
Beat	
	What the fuck was I sposed to do? I walked 'er to 'er door./ She told me about 'er 'usband an' 'er kids. / Ow she 'ad a night job cos 'er daughter was 'avin fuckin' ballet lessons. / I don't know what it was. / It just left me. / Dint wanna do it. / Dint wanna do it. Just one day an' I dint wanna do it. /
Beat	
	When we got to 'er door./ We said our goodbyes an' she thanked me. / What's she

Beat

fuckin' thankin' me for? / Thanked me./ Like 'er life depended on it.

A stranger is less human than someone you know.

Neil exits

ACT TWO SCENE ELEVEN

The Mother and The Father.
Pub. Day.
FX: Light change.

FATHER	No. Margaret. I'm not goin'.
MOTHER	Why not?
FATHER	It'll be all sympathetic nods an' 'andin' round the tissues.
MOTHER	That's not a good enough answer.
FATHER	I'm not payin' £30 an hour to whinge to a complete stranger.
MOTHER	It's free. Don't be so workin' class all your life.
FATHER	She'll be pickin' over me thoughts.
MOTHER	What all three of 'em.
FATHER	It's invasive.
MOTHER	It's not about your male pride. It's about us supportin' Tanya.
FATHER	Give me a fuckin' shot gun to blast at you know who. That'll be supportin' Tanya.

Pause

MOTHER	Don't swear. Ya know I don't like it when ya swear.

Beat

FATHER	What's in it for the 'do gooder?'
MOTHER	It's 'er job.
FATHER	Is she one of them femms?
MOTHER	*(Sighs)* Would it matter if she was?
FATHER	Well she can be as femm as she likes. But if my tea's not on the table when I get back from this nonsense.

ACT TWO SCENE TWELVE

Janet and Gary's flat. Morning.
FX: Lights up.

Janet is sat on the couch with Gary. Gary is massaging her feet

GARY	It's called a plea bargain.
JANET	Well I don't see why you 'ave to bargain for a plea if you've done fuck all wrong.
GARY	It's just the way the system works Janet. You plead guilty an' you get a more lenient sentence.
JANET	THAT FUCKIN' SHONA.
GARY	She's just a crazy bitch. Like the other one. Nobodies gonna believe a word they say.
JANET	Shit sticks.
GARY	If it ever gets to court, they'll rip 'er to pieces. 'Alf the towns bin through 'er.
JANET	Oh charmin'.
GARY	You know what I mean.
JANET	Yeah. I know what ya mean.

Beat

GARY	Don't let them bastards come between us. I need you on my side. Even my mams bin treatin' me like a prize cunt.

Beat

>Are we okay?

Pause

JANET   We're okay. Will you make me a cuppa tea an' get us one of them paracetamols out of the cupboard?

GARY   Yeah. Course I will. When this is all over, we'll set a new date for the weddin' an' we can get on wiv the rest of our lives.

JANET   Yeah.

He puts his arms around her waist

GARY   Ya know I don't always say it. But you know that I love you. Don't you?

He kisses her

JANET   Yeah. Go on. Where's me tea.

Gary exits. Janet relaxes on the couch

ACT TWO SCENE THIRTEEN

NEIL. (With his WENDY LETTERS)
SFX: 'Hey', THE PIXES.
FX: Spotlight on Neil.

NEIL   She had strength and vulnerability in equal measure.

Beat

That kind of mixture drives a man to distraction.

Beat

I often got the urge to punch the bitch off 'er pedestal. /

Pause

She cheated on me once. / The lyin' little fucker denied it. / So I called 'er over to mine for 'er tea. Before she got there I laid out all me old love letters from me ex's on the front room floor. /

Beat

She fuckin' waltzed in. Thinkin' she was The Queen of fuckin' Sheba. / WORLD STOP FOR ME. / I'VE ARRIVED. Then she started rippin' 'em up. / Rippin' up my fuckin' love letters. / Scatterin' my fuckin love letters all over my fuckin' 'ouse.

Beat

Now I'm not a violent man. But disrespectin' my ex birds. / I won't 'ave it./

An' she knew what she was doin'. / Pushin' my fuckin' buttons. / CUNT.

Beat

Sorry ladies. / That's an 'orrible word. I know. / I mean it's not an 'orrible thing. / It's a fuckin' honey pot. / The gift that keeps on givin'. / But it's an' 'orrible word.

Pause

She never liked Tash, an' 'e cunt stand the sight of 'er snide face. / Turned 'is back on 'er every time she came to the 'ouse. When I'd got 'er down on the floor. Ripped 'er pants off 'er bony fuckin' arse 'e knew what to do. / See they're clever like that dogs. / Not like fuckin' women. / My boy climbed on 'er back, slipped it in an' 'e dint even need to look at 'er sly face. The best of it is, whilst my boy was pumpin' away, I made the cheatin' bitch read my left over love letters. / It's true what they say? CUNTS always the first to be unfaithful.

Neil exits

ACT TWO SCENE FOURTEEN

Hospital. Day.
FX: Spotlight on Shona.

Shona is sat next to Girl 29 stage right. The Mother is sat stage left

SHONA The other day I was reading an article by Julie Birchall, and she wrote that, 'The modern day illness of the female is to pretend to be complex, or traumatised and that way she's deemed acceptable by society'. I don't feel very accepted by society and I don't pretend to be complex or traumatised. I'm quite straight forward really. I used to like Julie Birchall. But now I think she's been spending too much time hanging out in Notting Hill nail bars with high class prostitutes.

MOTHER I've bin tryin' to find a reason why this 'appened to my girl. But you know what? I can't find a single reason why. A world full of reasons and I can't find one.

SHONA The reasons don't lie within you me or Tanya. They lie within men who hate women. The men who did this to her.

MOTHER I don't believe any of that nonsense about sufferin' makin' you stronger.

SHONA   Neither do I. We're strong enough. I went to a psychic once and she told me that my soul was damaged. I thought she was talking rubbish. But that's what sexual abuse does. / It damages your soul, and you can carry it for lifetimes. Until you find a way to set yourself free.
MOTHER   Do you think they'll find 'im guilty?
SHONA   ?

FX: Lights fade.
SFX: 'Dare', JUNIOR SANCHEZ REMIX. (Continuous play)

ACT TWO SCENE FIFTEEN

Club. Night.

Gary dances and swigs from a bottle of beer
Neil approaches him with a bottle of beer.   They embrace
SFX: The Music lowers.

NEIL	What did they give ya?
GARY	All charges dropped.
NEIL	First offence and lack of evidence?
GARY	Sommat like that.
NEIL	Nice one. *(Pointing to audience member)* Check out the blonde. I'm gonna buy 'er drink.
GARY	Listen. Janet's pregnant so I think me an' you shud keep our distance for now.
NEIL	Did you say Janet's pregnant?
GARY	Yeah.
NEIL	Back of the net. Top shot. Home goal.
GARY	Eh.
NEIL	Don't get me wrong. No disrespect mate, but she must only 'ave about two eggs left. You're lucky you 'it the jackpot.
GARY	Well like I said. I think it's best that you an' me keep our distance. All this stuff with Tanya 'as knocked Janet for six. I've not seen 'er this upset for a long time.

NEIL	Yeah, yeah, alright. Spare me your personal problems. *(Holding up his beer)* Do you want another?
GARY	No mate, I'm gonna get off.
NEIL	So am I mate, with the blonde.

Neil exits into the audience
Gary swigs another mouthful of lager
He scans around the dance floor and then exits

SFX: Music Fades

Lights Fade

ACT TWO SCENE SIXTEEN

Janet and Gary's flat. Morning.
FX: Lights up.

Janet is asleep on the couch. Sheldon enters

SHELDON　　Janet.
JANET　　*(Startled)* You've got a nerve. Showin' your face in my 'ouse.
SHELDON　　I've bin meanin' to talk to ya.
JANET　　*(Sitting up)* Yeah. I've got fuck all to say to you.

Beat

SHELDON　　She's a kid. Decent people can't get their 'eads around what's 'appened.
JANET　　I'm not decent? Their twisted sense of morality says me an' Gary are scum?
SHELDON　　You lied for 'im Janet. /
JANET　　These are people who rip off the social. Sell drugs. Rob their own. /
SHELDON　　You lied Janet. You lied. /
JANET　　Yet they 'ave a fuckin' peckin'order on the hierarchy of crime. You can rob from your neighbour, but you can't fuck 'er.

Beat

SHELDON   It wasn't a fuck Janet.

Pause

JANET   Yeah. You're right. It wasn't a fuck. Because it wunt anythin', because it neva fuckin' 'append. An' my Gary's bin cleared. An' those fuckin' hypocrites, cos that's all they fuckin' are. They're gonna be apologisin'.
SHELDON   You're wrong Janet. You're wrong.

Silence
Sheldon exits. Janet exits

FX: Lights Fade

ACT TWO SCENE SEVENTEEN

Janet and Gary's flat.
SFX: 'That Was My Veil', PJ HARVEY.
FX: Single spot on Gary.

Music Fades
Gary alone

GARY   I'm glad I left the army. Janet always says that they brain washed me. She says it turned me into a social autistic, obsessed with routine. There was this one geezer I met in there. 'Gibbo'. Paul Gibbons. We used to call 'im 'The Ape', for obvious reasons. 'E was built like a brick shit 'ouse. Nobody fucked wiv Gibbo. Not unless they 'ad a 3 be 2 in their 'and.

Beat

There was this one night. We were on a night off an' went to one of the pubs by the barracks. There was this bird. / She was alright. All the squaddies used to take the piss out of 'er, cos she drank alone at the bar. Called 'er a prossie an' all that. She just liked a drink, like me ma. Think she liked the company. Nowt as sad as an old drunk, drinkin' on their own in the 'ouse.

Beat

Pause

    Well this one night, Gibbo, 'e'd 'ad a bit to drink like, an' 'e made this bet with the other squaddies that 'e cud chat 'er up, an' get 'er outside for a bit of 'ow's your father. True to Gibbo form, she fell for 'is smarm an' 'e got 'er outside.

    When we got outside 'e'd already got 'er pinned against the wall, 'er kecks around 'er ankles, an' the dirty bastard was rammin' 'er. I mean she dint seem to be mindin' it. / She was makin' a bit of noise at first, an' then she just relaxed into it and enjoyed it.

Pause

    The other lads all took turns an' that, an' they asked me to be look out. I think after a while she got a bit tired, cos she kept doin' this gaspin' thing. / Like you know she cunt breathe.

Pause

    I did tell the lads to lay off 'er a bit. / But you know? They were. /

(Beat. Janet enters. She is dressed in her night gown)

    When they'd finished, they fucked off back inside the pub. An' she just lay there wiv 'er blouse ripped an' 'er bits 'angin' out. She was sobbin' like a child sobs,

	when you punish it for bein' bad. She made no attempt to cover 'erself up. I tried to 'elp 'er, but she want 'avin' none of it.
JANET	You'll get locked away for that. /
GARY	*(Startled)* Eh.
JANET	Talkin' to yourself. Are you comin' to bed?

She kisses him and strokes his face

GARY	I'll be up in a minute.
JANET	Don't be long.

She exits

GARY	The truth is. / I think the army fucked me up. I deal with it better than I did. But the pictures in your memory, they never leave ya.

Gary exits

ACT TWO SCENE EIGHTEEN

Hospital. Night.
FX: Lights up on The Mother, The Father and Sheldon.

FATHER	It's a waste of time Margaret.
MOTHER	You're not dropping out after 2 sessions.
FATHER	It's not 'elpin' Tanya.
SHELDON	It will Mr 'udson. She's goin' through 'The Re-organisation Phase'. She's tryin' to make sense of everythin' that's 'appened to 'er.
FATHER	IT'S JUST TALKIN', TALKIN', BLOODY TALKIN'.
MOTHER	Oh an' what do you suggest?
FATHER	What would make me feel better is gettin' 'old of that fuckin' Gary.
MOTHER	Don't start all that again. You go round there shoutin' your mouth off an' you'll make the situation ten times worse.
FATHER	I've got a right to 'ear what 'e 'as to say for 'imself.
MOTHER	He's scum. It won't be worth 'earin'.
SHELDON	An' 'e's ex army. You don't want to be windin' 'im up while Janet's pregnant. 'E's got a terrible temper on 'im.

Beat

FATHER   I used to 'ave this naïve view that the law was there to protect people or at least grant 'em some form of justice.

SHELDON   My Tommy says the laws are there to grind the poor an' it's always the rich that make 'em.

FATHER   Do you know what 'urts the most? 'E's gonna do it again. E's just gonna go back out there an' do it to some other young girl.

Lights Fade
FX: Spot light on Sheldon

SHELDON   *(She addresses the parents)* I don't want to tell you this. *(Pause)* But I think you've got a right to know. *(Pause. She stands and addresses the audience)* When I started volunteering with the Street Angels I was told by a copper, (off record) that the Police 'ave about a week to deal with each rape when it's reported.

Beat

That means that if they think there's not enough evidence for a prosecution, within that first week, they may as well drop the case. If the victim's brave enough to push the case forward, the witness statements support the offenders' story.

Beat

(To the Mother and Father) I'm sorry. / I only saw Gary 'elpin' her into a taxi. I never saw him rapin' her. The copper told me about one drug rape that was filmed for fun by a door man, inside a night club. When they came to prosecute the offenders, they said the girl 'ad consented to 'ave sex with 'em an' that she was just drunk. When the coppers watched the film back, the girl just looked like she was.../ *(She bows her head in shame)* They got off with the rape.

Beat

With the police, it's all about keeping the stats down. They can get them for pimpin'. They can get them for kidnappin'. They can get them for robbin'. But they very rarely get them for rape.

Beat

(Angrily) IT'S LIKE RAPE DOESN'T EXIST. The rapists 'ave all the protection. Tanya's just another number.

ACT TWO SCENE NINETEEN

Janet and Gary's flat. Night.
SFX: 'Softly Softer', HOLE.
FX: Lights up on Janet.

Janet is rubbing cream into her arms
Gary is watching her

JANET   What are you looking at?
GARY   You.
JANET   What do you see when you look at me?
GARY   You.

Pause

JANET   Do you ever think of anybody else when we're 'avin' sex?
GARY   Why wud I do that?
JANET   I don't know. / But some guys do. / You know. / 'Ave their own little, private fantasy worlds goin' on, while they're fuckin' their wives girlfriends or whoever.
GARY   An' I'm sure some women do too.
JANET   I remember when I was datin' this guy from Iraq. We were walkin' down the road, holdin' hands, an' just before we passed the kebab shop 'e asked me to cross over the road. I asked 'im, 'What for?'. An' 'e said, 'because of 'im'. I looked

	across the road an' the guy in the kebab shop was lookin' at me with disgust. 'See', 'e said. 'I don't like the way 'e's lookin' at you. Because you're with me, 'e thinks you're a white slag'.
GARY	Well that's kendo for ya.
JANET	Don't call 'em that.
GARY	Pakis, Iraqis. I seen the way they treated their own women when I was over there.
JANET	I bet that's 'ow some porn models feel.
GARY	What?
JANET	When men look at 'em. I bet they feel like 'ow 'e made me feel. Like filth.

Gary hangs his head, sulkily

	What's the matter?
GARY	Nothin'.
JANET	You, looked dead sad. Will you rub some cream into my back?

Gary massages cream into Janet's back.

JANET	I think you're one of the few men that I've bin with, who actually likes women.
GARY	Why don't we move away? Get away from all this bullshit that's bin goin' on.
JANET	We can't just up an' go.

GARY   There's nothin' keepin' us 'ere. I can get a transfer with my job. You're always goin on about movin'.
JANET   It wunt be movin'. It wud be runnin' away.

Janet turns to face him

GARY   Like we give a shite about what the losers round 'ere think. Leave 'em to their warped gossip.
JANET   Is that what you really want?
GARY   I need to get away Janet. I feel hemmed in by everythin' that's 'appened.
JANET   If that's what you want, then we'll do it.

She moves in close to him and they kiss
SFX: of breaking glass

Gary exits onto the street, followed by Janet
The Father is stood outside and grabs hold of Gary

GARY   What the fuck are you doin'?
FATHER   You, you. / Despicable animal.
GARY   Get off me.
JANET   Get off 'im.
FATHER   Because of you my daughter says nowt, eats nowt an' plans nowt. /
JANET   'E neva did nothin', fuckin' get off 'im.

FATHER	All she does is sit an' stare out of an 'ospital winda all day. /
JANET	Please let go of 'im.
FATHER	'Ow wud you like someone to do that to your kid eh? This piece of shit is gonna be the father of your child, an' you protect 'im.
JANET	Please let him go.

The Father drags Gary by his neck and slams him against the wall and then pummels him with his fists
The Father pulls Gary's head back to finish him off with an upper cut to his chin

FX: Lights up on Girl 29 sewing. She stops suddenly.
FX: Lights up on Shona, sleeping on the chair. She bolts forward.

SHONA	*(Screaming)* NO…
GIRL 29	*(Screaming)* NO…

The Father lets go of Gary
Gary drops to the floor and Janet consoles him
FX: Blackout
FX: A slow release of very 'bright' light on the paintings of the 4 Girls. The light is intended to symbolise an 'awakening' or 'Angelic Presence'
SFX: (INTERLUDE) in between 'Doll Parts' and 'Credit In The Straight World' HOLE
The Father exits. Janet helps Gary to his feet and they exit

ACT THREE SCENE ONE

Shona's story. Night.

Shona walks, bare foot, to the centre of the stage, into the light. She is holding her shoes

SHONA   He'd been watching me. He knew that I never carried a bag with me. I was scared of being robbed. He was a neighbour. / Lived a couple of doors down. / Invited me in for a coffee. / Asked me to take my shoes off. / Very clean. / Said his sister had been raped, but no one had believed her. / Said he was looking after her. / That was good of him I thought. He believed that god was a black man, so I laughed and said, 'God, she's a black feminist woman'.

Beat

'Drink your coffee'. / 'It tastes funny', I said. My head was spinning. / I knew something wasn't right. / I felt panic in the pit of my stomach. *(She looks at her shoes)* I couldn't put them on quickly enough. 'Drink it', / he said. He held his fist up to my face. / He was getting angrier and angrier. / 'DRINK IT'. OR I'LL BREAK YOUR JAW'.

Beat

Pause

How could I fight the bastard? He tricked me. Paralysed me with drugs.

When I woke up. / I was on a bed. / He jumped off me. / His face etched with guilt. / He had stacks of porn. / He showed me one of the girls in the magazine. She looked just like me. / 'I watched this film once', he said. 'There was this girl gettin' done by three guys. She was lovin' it'. 'Really, was she' I said. 'Are you fuckin' sure about that?'

Beat

'You need to be taught a lesson', he said. 'You're just like Eva. / She was like you. / Ungrateful. / I looked after her. / Protected her. / Kept her safe. / She had a filthy mouth. Just like you'.

Beat

When I woke up, there was blood on the bed. He'd dressed me, but my under wear was missing. 'Where's my knickers?' I said. 'What do you want those for?' he said.

Beat

'They're mine. They belong to me'. 'Don't be so materialistic', he said. / Materialistic. / They were my knickers. / He was sat at the side of the bed, wringing his hands. /

Beat

'Can I go now?' I said. 'Not yet', he said.

Shona sits centre stage
FX: Lights fade.

ACT THREE SCENE TWO

Janet and Gary's flat. Day.
FX: Lights up.

Janet and Gary are loading up a van with the contents of their home
Gary enters with his arm in a sling
Janet enters

JANET	Last one. / Go on you. Get in the van. I'll get it. *(She signals to him to go)* Just give us five minutes.
GARY	Don't be long. This place gives me the creeps with nothin' in it.

Janet takes a deep breath and glances around the sitting room.
She picks up the final box then notices Gary's coat on the sofa.
She picks up Gary's coat
SFX: 'Phone ring tone'
She puts her hand into the coat pocket to retrieve the phone.
She pulls out the photograph of Gary with Girl 29
Her face slowly changes to a look of distress
She instinctively drops the box and clasps her hands over her mouth
FX: The lights fade slowly on Janet
FX: Lights rise slowly on Shona centre stage

ACT THREE SCENE THREE

Night.

SHONA 'Can I go now?' I said. 'Not yet', he said. / 'Not until you've told me the names and addresses of all your family and friends'. /

Pause

He wrote down every name. Every post code. He even asked me to spell some of them out. Then he turned to me and he said, / 'If you ever tell anyone what I did to you…/ *(She takes a deep breath)* I'll find you and I'll murder you and then I'll go back and find all your family and friends and I'll mur' / *(She clasps her mouth)* It took me a long time to say that in my counselling sessions.

Pause

I didn't realise what had happened until a week after. I kept getting terrifying flashbacks. One minute I was serving drinks at work. / The next minute. / I just collapsed. / Wiped out. / I had a nervous breakdown. / I was in hospital for 2 weeks. They sectioned me and put me on suicide watch. / The female psychiatrist said to me 'Do you feel like you've been raped more than once and by more than one person? / 'Yes', I said. 'I do'.

Pause

I had the best CPS Lawyer in the country working on my case. But they still couldn't get it to trial.

Pause

When I asked them why, they said it was because they didn't want to put me through any more mental distress. When the police raided the room, they found my missing underwear and the cups that he'd drugged me from. They still had my finger prints on them. Everything was just as I'd described it in my statement.

Pause

He'd not moved a thing. He imprisoned and raped me for nine hours and they let him walk away.

Pause

Sometimes, I dream that I'm back there. / I can feel them inside me. / Their heavy bodies on top of me. I can't move. I have to wait for them to STOP.

Pause

The dream always ends the same way. / Me / Flying barefoot. Above St Mary's in Manchester. / I'm free. / But I'm always holding my shoes.

She slowly offers her shoes to the audience
She sits down on the floor and then puts them on her feet
Lights Fade

ACT THREE SCENE FOUR

Janet's flat. Day.
FX: Lights up.

Shona enters. Janet is unpacking her personal items from a large box. The box reads 'STOP RUNNING'

JANET   Thanks for comin'. He's gone.

Pause

SHONA   I'm not a victim.

Janet turns to face Shona

JANET   I'm sorry.
SHONA   I'm a survivor.
JANET   I'm so sorry.
SHONA   No one believed me. They punished me. Locked me away. I had to hold it all inside.
JANET   I know.

Janet embraces her

SHONA   I just wanted them to know I was telling the truth.

Lights Fade

ACT THREE SCENE FIVE

Girl 29's house. Day.
FX: Lights up, on Shona and Girl 29.

GIRL 29   I never want it to 'appen to anyone else.

Beat

                 My councillor says there's no sacred place for rape victims to come together to grieve their losses.
SHONA   We're on a lonely path.

Beat

GIRL 29   Were you angry for a long time?
SHONA   Yes.
Pause
                 But then I forgave myself.

Girl 29 hands Shona her finished tapestry

GIRL 29   I'd like you to 'ave this.
SHONA   Thanks.
GIRL 29   It's girls' names. They're girls I know who've bin sexually assaulted or raped.

Girl 29 lays The Tapestry on the floor
Shona studies the words

SHONA   It reminds me of something Andrea Dworkin wrote in 'Heartbreak'. She said that every tear she cried had a name attached to it.
GIRL 29   It always seems so normal when they tell ya. Like we 'ave to expect that's what 'appens to us. But that's the thing. / At the same time, you never expect it to 'appen to you.

Beat

SHONA   I wish they didn't rape.
GIRL 29   So do I. What would you say to 'im if you saw 'im again?
SHONA   Nothing. It was just one day. He doesn't stop me from enjoying my life.

Beat
Shona stares furtively at Girl 29

GIRL 29   What. / What are you lookin' at me like that for?
SHONA   Like what?
GIRL 29   *(Wiggling her finger)* Like, 'You've got a lot to learn young lady'.
SHONA   Don't you just hate it when us crusty old femms do that?

Beat

	It's like looking back into a mirror, when I was 18. / You remind me of what I lost.
Pause	
	What time's your mum back?

Shona puts on her coat

GIRL 29	I don't know. Will you come and see me again?

Shona smiles

SHONA	Try and stop me.

ACT THREE SCENE SIX

Park. Day.
SFX: 'Sketch for Summer', THE DURITTI COLUMN.
FX: The lights are bright to accentuate a sunny day.

Sheldon packs a picnic basket
Shona hangs her tapestry up on her wall
Janet continues unpacking her personal belongings and places them back in her flat
The Girls meet in the street
Janet and Sheldon carry the basket
Shona follows behind

SFX: The music fades.

JANET	I said a fuckin' cooler bag from the Asda. Not a fuckin' pet basket.
SHELDON	Ah. / It's not that big.
JANET	It's fuckin' huge. We looked like the famous five gettin' off that bus.
SHELDON	*(To Shona)* That's what I wanted to ask ya. You know that all the old femms fought for equality and our right to vote. / *(To Janet)* Do you vote?
JANET	Do I fuck. They're all wankers.
SHELDON	Yeah. / They fought for our right to vote an' other stuff. What do the new femms fight for?
SHONA	It's a post-modern, individualistic thing.

Sheldon and Janet glance at each other

JANET Why be obscure, when you can be really fuckin' obscure.
SHELDON Do you wanna elaborate on that?
SHONA It's not that the personal is the political. It's just that there's more. HIV. Trafficking. Enforced marriages. Slavery. Biological warfare. There's lots to do you know.
JANET Might as well slit me wrists now then.
SHONA We need to keep the faith.
JANET *(Sarcastically)* Rock on sista.
SHONA We need to be constantly vigilant.

SFX: Workman whistles and cat calls

JANET Oh there's the fuckin' wildlife. Right on que. I'm 30 fuckin 8. When does it end? When me tits are on the floor.

Sheldon quickens her pace

SHELDON Oh come on. Let's 'urry up. I can't be arsed with this. You'd think they'd 'ave more creative ways of gettin' our attention.
WORKMAN1 *(To Sheldon)* Easy does it love. You'll be warmin' your water if you go any faster.

Sheldon slams the basket down on the floor
She marches towards the audience and addresses The Worky

SHELDON   YEAH. WELL. YOU WON'T BE SCALDIN' YOUR COCK IN IT.

Shona and Janet join Sheldon in 'vigilant', sisterly solidarity

JANET   OI, YOU.
SHELDON   YEAH, YOU. WE'RE TALKIN' TO YOU.
SHONA   DO YOU THINK IT'S ACCEPTABLE TO HARASS WOMEN WHEN THEY'RE WALKING DOWN THE ROAD? /
JANET   MINDING THEIR OWN BUSINESS? /
WORKMAN1   ?
SHONA   Well. We're waiting.
WORKMAN2   It was 'im.
SHELDON   We know who it was. Shitbag.
SHONA   And I think your employer would be interested to know what you do during your working hours.
SHELDON   If we see or 'ear you harassin' any female that walks down this street again, you'll be whistlin' at the back of the dole queue. Okay.

Workman 1 and 2 stand gobsmacked

JANET   Classless Tramps. Suck my fuckin' left one.

The Girls walk away

SHELDON   We scared the shit out of 'em. That one's checkin' if 'is balls are still there.
JANET   'E's lucky e's still got any balls left.

The Girls find a comfy spot of grass and sit down
Sheldon unpacks the 'pet basket'
She hands sandwiches to Janet and Shona
She pulls out a bottle of wine from the basket

SHELDON   Look what I found.
SHONA   You two really need to cultivate your taste in fine wines.
SHELDON   I cunt give a shit about knowin' me Beaujolais from my brie.
JANET   *(Swigging from the bottle)* 'Ere, 'ere. The only thing I give a shit about is what gets me pissed quickest for under a fiver.

The girls sit back and relax

SHONA   It's such a lovely day.

Beat

SHELDON   What are you gonna tell the baby about 'er dad, when she's old enough?

JANET	The truth. Why would I want to tell 'er anythin' else. /
SHONA	Yeah. It takes a city of women to nail a rapist. *(Pulling out a letter from her bag)* I got this today. It's about my case. They've put it up for review.

She hands the letter to Sheldon

	I'm going to go for it again. I need to fight it.
SHELDON	Why keep torturin' yourself. It's like a scab. / If you keep pickin' at it, it won't heal.
JANET	If she needs to fight it, let 'er. Some battles are worth fighting for.

Pause

Just make sure that this time. / YOU GET THAT CUNT.

Neil enters and watches the girls
Play out with 'Carnival', NATALIE MERCHANT

Fade Out

THE END